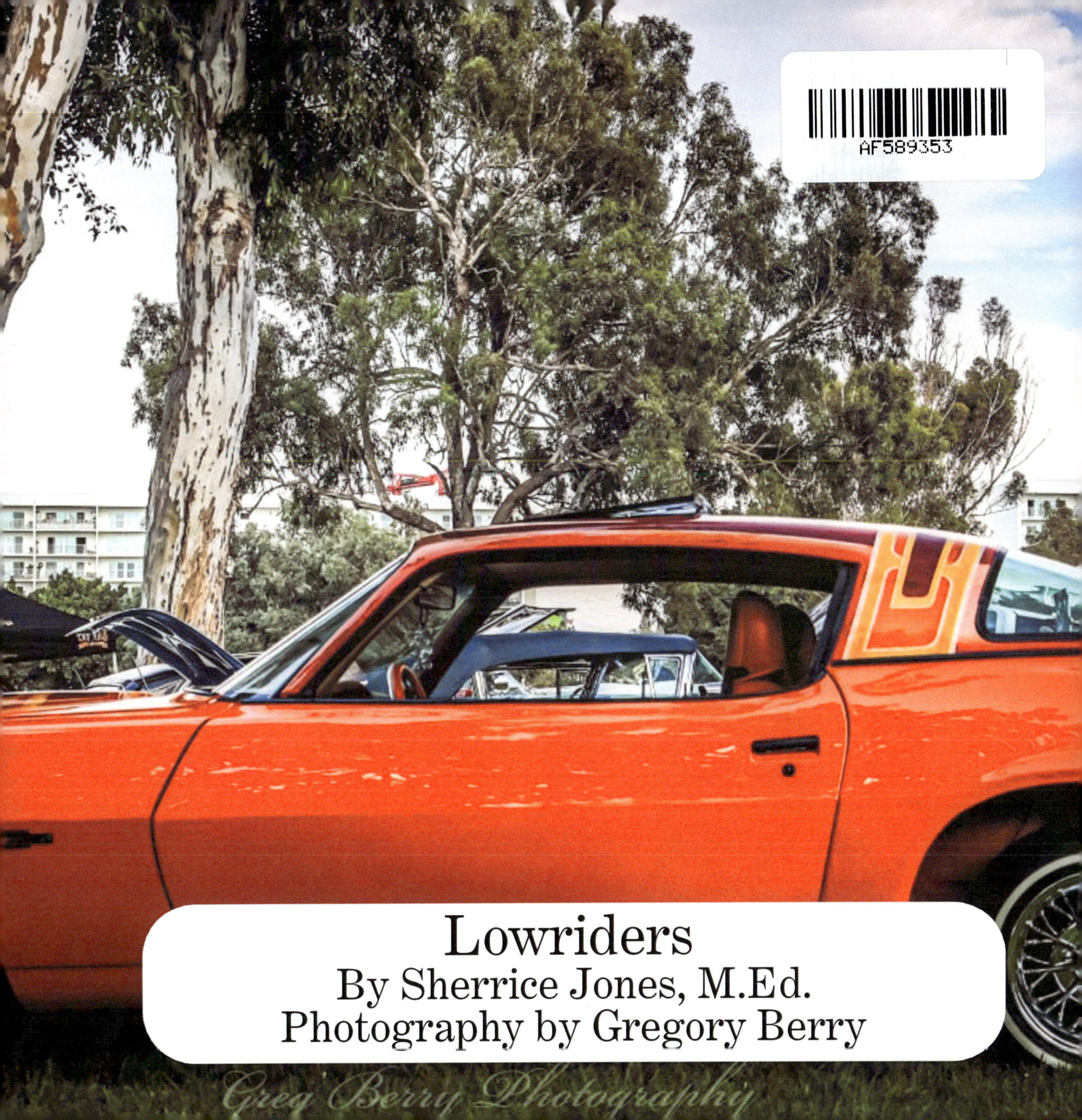

Lowriders

By Sherrice Jones, M.Ed.

Photography by Gregory Berry

Written and Published by: Sherrice Jones
Pictures by Greg Berry Photography

Reading lessons for this book

ow Words

cow - down

snow - low/slow/show

long e Sound

tree - teens/see/wheels

eat - dream/steal

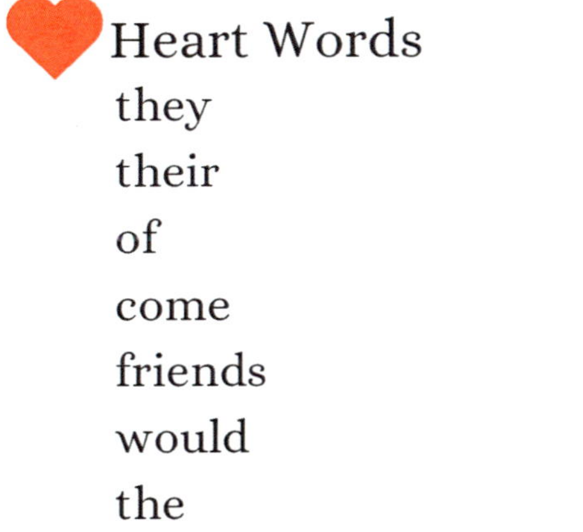

Heart Words

they
their
of
come
friends
would
the

Sight Words

and	that
go	but
up	not
make	it
down	help
like	in

Word Division

his-to-ry
glit-ter
re-mark-able

Syllable Types

R-controlled	Consonant 'le
car	sparkle
art	remarkable
sparkle	
remarkable	

Most kids dream of fixing a car to make it go fast, but not these teens.

With the help of their friends, they make cars sparkle. It's remarkable!

These cars are called Lowriders. They are a sight to see.

They have bright paint jobs and lots of chrome.

The wheels can go up.

The wheels can come down.

They make cars that hop and dance.

People like to see them when they get a chance.

They make cars that glitter and glow.

They make cars that steal the show!

Some use them to stay cool and hide.

Some make cars to express their pride.

They make cars that go low, low, low.

They make cars that go low and slow.

They make cars to show their style.

They make cars to have fun.

They make cars that tell a story.

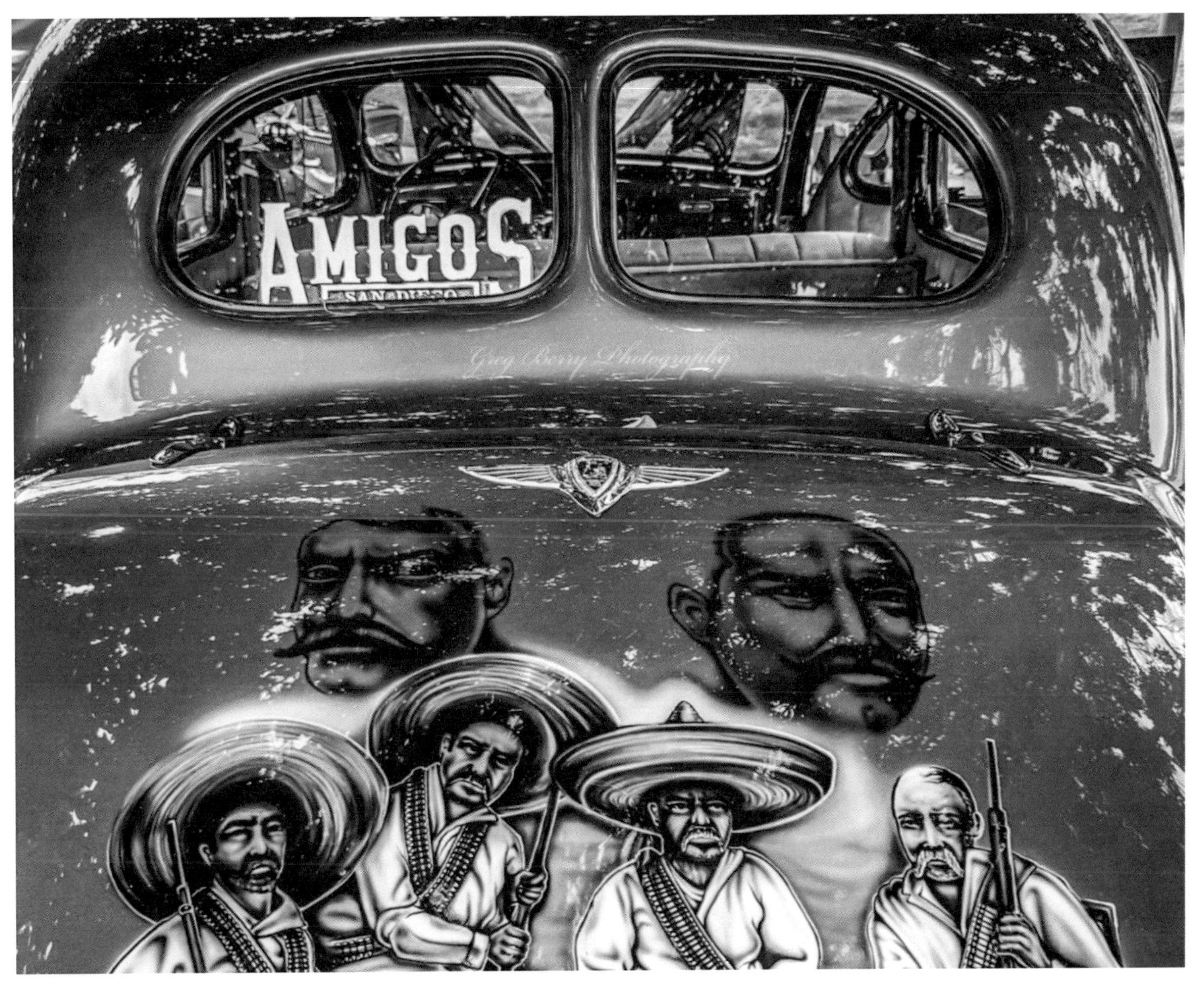

They make cars that tell their history.

Lowriders are a part of Hispanic culture. The cars are like moving art.

Would you like to ride in a Low rider?

www.ingramcontent.com/pod-product-compliance
Ingram Content Group UK Ltd.
Pitfield, Milton Keynes, MK11 3LW, UK
UKRC032027290726
14090UKWH00008B/487